CHRISTMAS MAGIC

Holiday Magic Books

Christmas
MAGIC

by James W. Baker
pictures by George Overlie

Lerner Publications Company Minneapolis

To my son, Glenn, a jolly elf who enjoys the magic in the air at Christmas time. As a youngster, he was levitated, sawed in half, and vanished, all in the interest of improving my magic act, and he never once complained.

This book is available in two editions:
Library binding by Lerner Publications Company
Soft cover by First Avenue Editions
241 First Avenue North
Minneapolis, Minnesota 55401

Library of Congress Cataloging-in-Publication Data
Baker, James W., 1926-
   Christmas magic/by James W. Baker; pictures by George Overlie.
     p.   cm.—(The Holiday magic books)
   Summary: Explains how to perform ten magic tricks revolving around
a Christmas theme.
   ISBN 0-8225-2227-6 (lib. bdg.)
   ISBN 0-8225-9537-0 (pbk.)
   1. Tricks—Juvenile literature. 2. Christmas—Juvenile
literature. [1. Magic tricks, 2. Christmas.] I. Overlie,
George, ill. II. Title. III. Series: Baker, James W., 1926-
Holiday magic books.   88-2703
GV1548.B333   1988   CIP
793.8—dc19   AC
Manufactured in the United States of America

1 2 3 4 5 6 7 8 9 10 97 96 95 94 93 92 91 90 89 88

CONTENTS

INTRODUCTION

At Christmastime, families decorate sweet-smelling pine trees with ornaments and tinsel. The smells of cookies and cider and cinnamon hang in the air. Grandparents and cousins surround a table piled high with food. Carolers sing under a starry sky.

Christmas is a time for giving and receiving gifts. On Christmas Eve, children throughout the world wait by a window, hoping to hear the sound of Santa's sleighbells or catch a glimpse of a reindeer's glowing red nose.

In the magical spirit of the holiday, you can present your friends and family with a Christmas magic show. Learn to perform the magic tricks in this book, and you can give magical gifts not only at Christmastime, but throughout the year.

A CHRISTMAS SPELL

HOW IT LOOKS

Lying on a table are some pictures associated with Christmas: Santa, ice, toys, reindeer, wreaths, and lights. You ask a volunteer from the audience to select one of the pictures. Without telling anyone which picture she chose, she then turns around so she can't see what you are doing. The rest of the audience watches you. You begin tapping the pictures, saying "Go" with each tap. The volunteer mentally spells the name of the picture she selected, one letter for each tap, and says "Stop" when she reaches the final letter. She tells the audience which picture she chose, then she turns around. The entire audience sees that you are pointing to the picture she mentally selected.

figure 1.

HOW TO MAKE IT

Cut out of a magazine or draw six pictures of a Santa, ice, toys, reindeer, wreaths, and lights (**Figure 1**). Label each picture exactly as listed. Once you have labeled all six pictures (and know the secret from the section on HOW TO DO IT) you are ready to perform this baffling trick.

Note that each picture used in the trick is spelled with a different number of letters: I-C-E = 3 letters, T-O-Y-S = 4 letters, S-A-N-T-A = 5 letters, L-I-G-H-T-S = 6 letters, W-R-E-A-T-H-S = 7 letters, and R-E-I-N-D-E-E-R = 8 letters.

1. Lay the labeled pictures haphazardly on the table, not in the order above.

2. Tap any pictures for the first two taps. Then tap ice for Number 3, toys for Number 4, Santa for Number 5, lights for Number 6, and so on. This will automatically complete the spelling on the chosen object.

A picture of another object can be substituted, as long as it has the same number of letters as the object it replaces, such as SNOW for 4, CANDY for 5, PRESENT for 7, ORNAMENT for 8, etc.

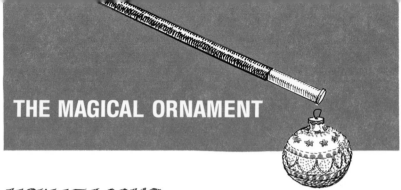

THE MAGICAL ORNAMENT

HOW IT LOOKS

Show a small Christmas ornament to your audience and explain that it has magical powers.
Then take a sheet of paper and tear it into three
pieces. Have one volunteer from the audience
write "Santa Claus" on one piece of paper, a second
volunteer write "Easter Bunny" on another piece
of paper, and a third volunteer write "Tooth Fairy"
on the last piece of paper. Have the three volunteers fold their papers once and drop them
into a paper bag marked "Santa's Toy Bag." Have
another volunteer blindfold you. Explain that
the magical Christmas ornament will help you
find the slip of paper marked "Santa Claus."

You reach into the bag with the ornament in your hand and bring out one of the three slips of paper. It is the one marked "Santa Claus." It has been located by the magical Christmas ornament.

HOW TO MAKE IT

For this trick, you will need a small Christmas ornament, a sheet of paper, a pencil, a paper bag marked "Santa's Toy Bag," and a scarf for a blindfold.

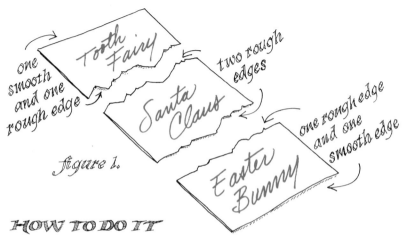

one smooth and one rough edge

Tooth Fairy

two rough edges

Santa Claus

one rough edge and one smooth edge

Easter Bunny

figure 1.

HOW TO DO IT

The "magical" Christmas ornament has nothing to do with locating the slip with "Santa Claus" written on it, but is used only for what magicians call *misdirection*, which takes the minds of the audience off the real method for doing the trick.

1. When you tear the sheet of paper into three pieces, you will note that the center piece has *two* rough edges while the top and the bottom pieces have only *one* rough edge (**Figure 1**).

2. Hand the center piece (with two rough edges) to a volunteer from the audience and tell him to write "Santa Claus" on his piece of paper.

3. Hand the other two pieces of paper (with only one rough edge) to the other two volunteers and tell them to write "Easter Bunny" and "Tooth Fairy" on their sheets.

4. Have the volunteers fold their sheets and drop them all into the bag.

5. When you reach into the bag you can easily tell which sheet is marked "Santa Claus" by feeling for the piece of paper with the two rough edges. You have to be a good actor when doing this trick, making the audience believe that it is the magical Christmas ornament—and not you—that is finding the "Santa Claus" paper.

THE VANISHING SANTA

HOW IT LOOKS

At the beginning of the trick, a clear water glass is upside-down on a sheet of white paper. You cover the glass with a cone-shaped paper Santa Claus hat. Place a small picture of Santa Claus on the white sheet of paper alongside the glass. Then lift the glass together with the cone-shaped Santa Claus hat and place both over the small picture of Santa Claus (Figure 1).

figure 1.

figure 2.

You say the magic word "Doog Leon"— Good Noel spelled backward—and lift the cone-shaped Santa Claus hat, leaving the glass upside-down over the small picture of Santa Claus. The picture has vanished (Figure 2).

Again placing the Santa Claus hat over the glass, you lift both the hat and the glass and the small picture of Santa Claus reappears (Figure 3).

figure 3.

HOW TO MAKE IT

The secret is in the glass, although the audience does not realize this.

1. You must prepare the glass ahead of time. Glue or paste a circular white paper disk to the top of the glass. Trim the edges of the paper so that it does not extend beyond the rim of the glass (**Figure 4**). When the glass is turned upside down on another piece of white paper the paper disk becomes invisible.

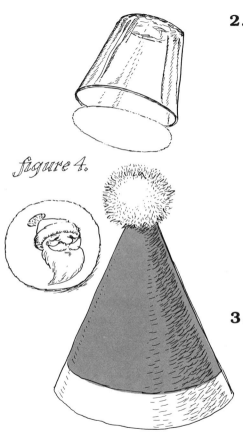

figure 4.

2. Glue a piece of red construction paper in the shape of a cone. Add a strip of white paper to the bottom of the cone and a ball of cotton to the point to make a Santa Claus hat. This hat should be big enough to just cover the glass.

3. Draw a small picture of Santa Claus on a piece of paper smaller than the top of the glass.

19

HOW TO DO IT

You will see that when you place the glass with the paper disk over the small picture of Santa Claus, the picture immediately vanishes because it is covered by the white paper disk pasted over the mouth of the glass. The cone-shaped Santa Claus hat over the glass hides the paper disk as you pick up the glass. When you lift the glass (with the Santa Claus hat) from the paper again, the small picture of Santa reappears.

CARD OF
CHRISTMAS SYMBOLS

HOW IT LOOKS

Show a mysterious-looking card of Christmas symbols to your audience. Then, without letting the audience see what you are writing, write a prediction on a piece of paper, fold it, and put it on a table in full view of the audience.

Ask a volunteer to call out a number from 1 to 16. Hand him the card of Christmas symbols. Ask him to turn the card so that the Christmas tree with his number on it is at the top of the card. Starting at the top, have him count the symbols from left to right, top row to bottom row—just as he would read a book—until he counts to his number. After he sees the symbol he landed on, have him read the prediction you wrote down at the beginning of the trick. You have correctly predicted the symbol he would land on, even though you had no idea which number he would choose.

HOW TO MAKE IT

For this trick, you will need a pencil, a piece of paper, and the card of Christmas symbols (**Figure 1**). Trace the card of Christmas symbols or redraw it *exactly* as shown.

figure 1.

23

HOW TO DO IT

The card of Christmas symbols is designed so that all 16 symbols look different. No one will notice that four of the symbols—although not exactly the same—are Christmas ornaments. When you make your prediction write "You will choose Christmas ornaments" on the slip of paper. No matter what number is chosen from 1 to 16 the volunteer will always land on one of the four symbols of Christmas ornaments.

HOW IT LOOKS

You place your hand flat on a table, palm down, and slide eight or ten Christmas cards underneath your palm. You then wave a magic Christmas wand and slowly lift the hand with the Christmas cards under it. The cards rise with your hand, defying gravity.

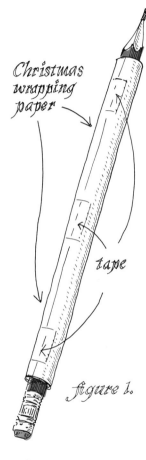

Christmas
wrapping
paper

tape

figure 1.

HOW TO MAKE IT

1. You will need to make a magic Christmas wand by rolling some rather stiff Christmas wrapping paper around a pencil and taping it in place (**Figure 1**). Remove the pencil.

2. You will also need eight or ten Christmas cards, a toothpick, and a ring that is somewhat loose on your finger.

HOW TO DO IT

1. Secretly slide the toothpick under your ring on the palm side. Slide the first two Christmas cards under your hand and above the toothpick to secure them (**Figure 2**).

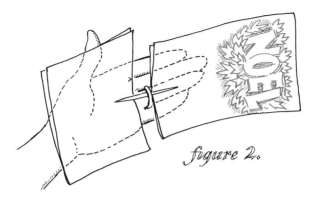

figure 2.

2. Slide the rest of the Christmas cards between your hand and the first two cards.

3. When you have slid all of the cards under your hand, slowly raise your hand, palm down. The cards will rise, clinging to your hand as if by magic. Next, slowly lower your hand to the table and remove the Christmas cards one by one.

4. Ask someone in the audience to examine the cards. While attention is focused on the Christmas cards, casually put your hand in your pocket and get rid of the toothpick.

THE RESTORED CHRISTMAS TREE

HOW IT LOOKS

Show a letter-size envelope to the audience and then seal it. With a pair of scissors, snip off the two ends. After showing a Christmas tree of green construction paper to the audience, push it into one end of the envelope until the top of the tree emerges from the other end. You then apparently cut the envelope and the tree inside in half, but when the Christmas tree is pulled out, it is obviously uncut.

HOW TO MAKE IT

1. Before you present this trick, and unknown to the audience, cut two slits in the back of the envelope (**Figure 1**).

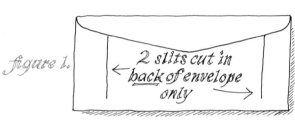

figure 1.

2 slits cut in
←back of envelope
only →

2. You will also need to make a long, thin Christmas tree out of green construction paper (**Figure 2**). It would be a good idea to glue two pieces together so the tree is stiff. Make sure that it is not too wide to go through the two slits in the envelope.

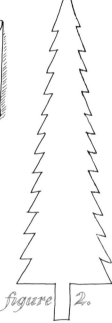

figure 2.

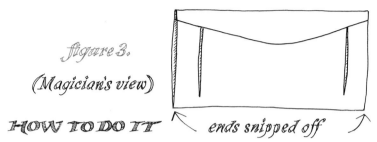

figure 3.

(Magician's view)

HOW TO DO IT ↖ *ends snipped off* ↗

1. Show the envelope, seal it, and snip off the two ends (**Figure 3**).
2. Insert the Christmas tree in the envelope. Make sure it comes out of one slit and goes back in the other instead of going straight through.

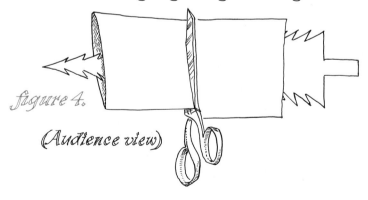

figure 4.

(Audience view)

3. When you cut the envelope in half, bend the
   envelope and insert the scissors between the
   Christmas tree and the envelope so that the tree
   remains undamaged (**Figure 4** and **Figure 5**).
Practice this in front of a mirror until you are
certain the audience cannot see the tree as you
cut the envelope.

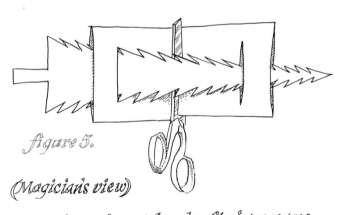

figure 5.

(Magician's view)

scissors inserted <u>under</u> Christmas tree

CHRISTMAS MIND READING

HOW IT LOOKS

You put a Christmas card, a Christmas ornament, and a Christmas candle on a table and
invite a volunteer from the audience to touch
one of the objects while you are out of the room.
When you return, you take the person's hand
and say something like "Please concentrate on
the item you touched." Close your eyes. "I am
beginning to pick up your thoughts." You open
your eyes and touch the object that she touched
while you were out of the room.

HOW TO MAKE IT

For this trick, you will need a Christmas card, an ornament, a candle, and the secret described below.

HOW TO DO IT

A *confederate* is what magicians call a friend who helps you with the trick unknown to the audience. (Note: As a magician, the occasional use of a confederate is all right, but you should not over-use this method, or your audience might suspect that you always use a confederate.) In this trick, your friend, the confederate, signals to you which is the proper object.

1. He touches his left ear if the selected object is to his left.
2. He touches his right ear if the selected object is to his right.
3. If the object that was touched is in the center, he doesn't touch either ear.

THE MAGICIAN'S CHRISTMAS TREE

HOW IT LOOKS

Tell a story something like "It was Christmas time. One family in town was too poor to buy a Christmas tree. Along came a magician who created a magical Christmas tree for them from a roll of old newspapers." As you tell the story, show a batch of old newspapers all rolled up. With a pair of scissors, make four cuts in one end of the roll. Pull the center of the newspapers up to form a "Christmas tree" that is over six feet (2 m) tall.

HOW TO MAKE IT

Paste six or seven full sheets of newspaper together end-to-end to make one long strip of newspaper. Roll this long strip loosely into a tube about two inches (5 cm) in diameter. Put a rubber band around each end of the tube to keep it from unrolling (**Figure 1**).

HOW TO DO IT

1. As you tell the story from the section on HOW IT LOOKS, take the rubber band off the top of the roll of newspapers.
2. With the scissors, make four six-inch (15-cm) cuts in the top of the roll (**Figure 2**).

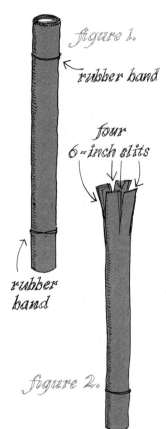

figure 1.

← *rubber band*

four 6-inch slits

rubber band

figure 2.

3. Bend the torn parts over, letting them fall outside the tube (**Figure 3**).

4. Reach inside the tube with your fingers and slowly pull up the center coils a little at a time, holding the roll of newspapers steady as you do. Gradually work the center of the coil up and up until you have a "Christmas tree" that is about six feet (2 m) high (**Figure 4**).

figure 3.

figure 4.

HOW IT LOOKS

Place pictures of a Christmas tree, a snowman, a Christmas candle, and a Christmas ornament on a large picture of Santa Claus. Have a volunteer from the audience select one of the four pictures. When the volunteer turns the large picture of Santa over, she finds that Santa Claus had predicted ahead of time which of the four pictures she would select.

HOW TO MAKE IT

1. For this trick, you will need to draw a picture of Santa Claus on a piece of construction paper (**Figure 1**). The picture should be at least eight inches (20 cm) high. On the back of the Santa Claus, print: "Ho. Ho. Ho. I knew you would pick the snowman. Santa Claus."

figure 1.

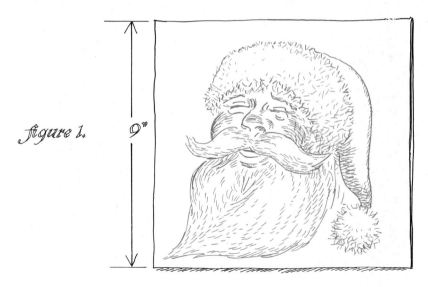

2. From white paper or cardboard, make four little round disks about two inches (5 cm) across. On one draw a Christmas tree, on another a snowman, on the third a Christmas candle, and on the last a Christmas ornament (**Figure 2**).

figure 2.

|← 2" →|

HOW TO DO IT

1. Place the picture of Santa Claus on the table, making sure no one sees what is written on the back.

2. Mix up the four round pictures and place one on each of Santa's eyes, one on his mouth, and one on the ball at the end of his cap. It doesn't matter which one goes where.

39

You will *force* the volunteer to select the snowman by the way you tell her what to do.

3. First, have her pick up any two of the round pictures.

a. If one of the two pictures she picks up is the snowman, you remove the other two pictures and set them aside, saying "We won't need these." Then you ask the volunteer to hand you one of the two pictures she picked up.

b. If she hands you the snowman, say "Fine!" and tell her to discard the other picture in her hand. Then you turn over the picture of Santa Claus with one hand and hold the snowman picture in the other.

c. If she hands you the other picture, you set that one aside with the other two discarded pictures and say, "Fine! That leaves you with the snowman." Then you turn over the picture of Santa Claus. Either way, Santa Claus has correctly predicted the snowman.

4. On the other hand, if the volunteer does not pick up the snowman when you ask her to pick up any two pictures, follow these steps.

a. You say, "OK, we'll get rid of these," as you set the two pictures that she picked up aside. Then you have the volunteer pick up the other two pictures—one of them being the snowman— and hand one to you.

b. If she hands you the snowman, you tell her to discard the other picture. Then you turn over Santa Claus with one hand, holding the snowman in the other hand.

c. If she hands you the other picture, set it aside and say, "Fine! That leaves you with the snowman." Then you turn over the picture of Santa Claus to reveal his prediction. Either way, Santa Claus has correctly predicted the snowman.

**TEN PRESENTS
FOR TWO DAUGHTERS**

HOW IT LOOKS

Tell a story something like "Two magicians had two daughters, Holly and Mistletoe. These parents loved their daughters equally and always tried to treat them equally as well. One Christmas, after all the presents were wrapped, the magicians discovered they had six presents for one daughter and only four for the other." You show the audience a picture of presents to illustrate this. "Being magicians, the parents knew how to solve the problem." You then demonstrate what they did. With a pair of scissors, cut the picture and rearrange the pieces. "Now, instead of six presents of one kind and four of the other, there are five of one kind and five of the other. Magically, the two daughters are treated equally."

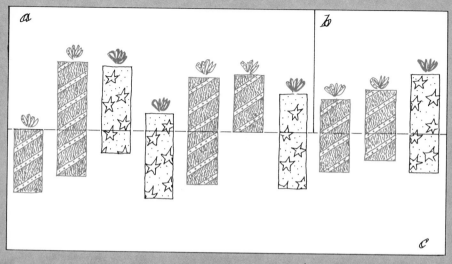

figure 1.

HOW TO MAKE IT

In **Figure 1** you see that there are 10 presents
in the picture, six of one kind (the dark ones)
and four of another kind (the light ones). Every
time you do the trick, trace **Figure 1** or redraw
it *exactly* as shown. You will also need a pair
of scissors.

44

HOW TO DO IT

1. Tell the story about the magicians and their two daughters. As you show the picture, point out that there are six dark presents and four light ones.

2. With a pair of scissors, cut the picture into three pieces (A, B, and C) along the horizontal and vertical lines.

3. Rearrange the three pieces by switching piece A and piece B.

4. Now count the presents. You will find that, magically, there are now five dark presents and five light ones. Even you, the magician, might not know how this happened.

TRICKS FOR BETTER MAGIC

Here are some simple rules you should keep in mind while learning to perform the tricks in this book.

1. Read the entire trick several times until you thoroughly understand it.
2. Practice the trick alone or in front of a mirror until you feel comfortable doing the trick, then present it to an audience.
3. Learn to perform one trick perfectly before moving on to another trick. It is better to perform one trick well than a half dozen poorly.
4. Work on your "presentation." Make up special "patter" (what you say while doing a trick) that is funny and entertaining. Even the simplest trick becomes magical when it is properly presented.
5. Choose tricks that suit you and your personality. Some tricks will work better for you than others.

Stick with these. *Every* trick is not meant to be performed by *every* magician.

6. Feel free to experiment and change a trick to suit you and your unique personality so that you are more comfortable presenting it.

7. Never reveal the secret of the trick. Your audience will respect you much more if you do not explain the trick. When asked how you did a trick, simply say "by magic."

8. Never repeat a trick for the same audience. If you do, you will have lost the element of surprise and your audience will probably figure out how you did it the second time around.

9. Take your magic seriously, but not yourself. Have fun with magic and your audience will have fun along with you.

ABOUT THE AUTHOR

James W. Baker, a magician for over 30 years, has performed as "Mister Mystic" in hospitals, orphanages, and schools around the world. He is a member of the International Brotherhood of Magicians and the Society of American Magicians, and is author of *Illusions Illustrated*, a magic book for young performers.

From 1951 to 1963, Baker was a reporter for *The Richmond (VA) News Leader*. From 1963 to 1983, he was an editor with the U.S. Information Agency, living in Washington, D.C., India, Turkey, Pakistan, the Philippines, and Tunisia, and traveling in 50 other countries. Today Baker and his wife, Elaine, live in Williamsburg, Virginia, where he performs magic and writes for the local newspaper, *The Virginia Gazette*.

ABOUT THE ARTIST

George Overlie is a talented artist who has illustrated numerous books. Born in the small town of Rose Creek, Minnesota, Overlie graduated from the New York Phoenix School of Design and began his career as a layout artist. He soon turned to book illustration and proved his skill and versatility in this demanding field. For Overlie, fantasy, illusion, and magic are all facets of illustration and have made doing the Holiday Magic books a real delight.